IONA DAWN

IONA DAWN

THROUGH HOLY WEEK WITH
THE IONA COMMUNITY

Neil Paynter (ed)

WILD GOOSE PUBLICATIONS

First published 2006 by
Wild Goose Publications,
4th Floor, Savoy House, 140 Sauchiehall St, Glasgow G2 3DH, UK.
Wild Goose Publications is the publishing division of the Iona Community.
Scottish Charity No. SCO03794. Limited Company Reg. No. SCO96243.
www.ionabooks.com

ISBN 1-905010-11-7
13-digit ISBN: 978-1-905010-11-0

Cover photo © Joy Mead
Cover design © Wild Goose Publications

A catalogue record for this book is available from the British Library.

Overseas distribution:
Australia: Willow Connection Pty Ltd, Unit 4A, 3-9 Kenneth Road,
Manly Vale, NSW 2093
New Zealand: Pleroma, Higginson Street, Otane 4170, Central Hawkes Bay
Canada: Novalis/Bayard Publishing & Distribution, 10 Lower Spadina Ave.,
Suite 400, Toronto, Ontario M5V 2Z2

Permission to reproduce any part of this work in Australia or New Zealand
should be sought from Willow Connection.

Printed by Bell & Bain, Thornliebank, Glasgow

CONTENTS

So we bless you for this place.

For your directing of us, Your redeeming of us,

and your indwelling …

George MacLeod, from
'A temple not made with hands'

INTRODUCTION

Neil Paynter

SETTING OUT (IONA 2000)

We got up while it was still dark
and gathered in Cul Shuna*
to say goodbye to Martina,
Kieran,
Maya,
Rahim,
Sarah and Maggie,
Jack and Dot and
Billy.

We held a service in the living room
out of the *Iona Abbey Worship Book*.

During the prayers we gave thanks to God for our time together
and asked Jesus to be with everyone on the road.

In silence we held hands …
then sang Sent by the Lord am I.
At breakfast,
Kieran was saying that he would be working in a homeless shelter
in Glasgow.

Maggie said she was going back to school
to be a midwife.
Dot and Jack were opening a house of welcome for asylum seekers
   and refugees.

I asked Billy what he was going to do.

He said he wasn't sure,
it hadn't really dawned on him yet –
but he knew it would,
in time.
He'd follow his heart.
He'd learned to do that here,
follow his heart.
It was the same as following Jesus, Billy said.

Helen called that the ferry was coming!
We ate our toast on the run.
Someone said:
Jesus was already on the ferry.

Kieran said, no –
he was probably halfway to Glasgow by now.

At the jetty we hugged and
said we'd keep in touch –
the air was salty
seabirds cried –
it felt like hell.
The ferry pulled away –

We stood in a long line
and did the Mexican wave;
sang again.

Our friends waved back.
Billy blew us a big kiss – and we all laughed.
Then gradually

in ones
and twos
and threes

Martina and
Kieran and
Maya and
Rahim and

Sarah and Maggie and
Jack and Dot
and Billy

turned to face the sunrise
                    coming up
over the mountains of Mull.

When I left Iona, after four difficult, wonderful years, I knew the challenge for me would be to find God on the mainland. When I left Iona a new time of my life was dawning. 'Morning had broken'. I felt the light on my face; it wasn't strong. It took me some time to know what to do with my life. For a while I did the same old thing; lived the same way.

This is a book by folk who have 'left' Iona, who are living and working on the mainland. Leith Fisher is a minister in Glasgow; Jan Sutch Pickard, ex-warden of

Iona Abbey and deputy warden at the MacLeod Centre, has been recently working in the West Bank; Tom Gordon is a chaplain at the Marie Curie hospice in Edinburgh; Brian Woodcock, ex-warden of Iona Abbey, is a URC minister in St Alban's; Peter Millar has been working with the Wellspring Community in Australia and with an AIDS project in Guguletu, South Africa – in February he is off to Brazil; Kathy Galloway is the leader of the Iona Community in Glasgow; Ruth Burgess is a writer who lately worked with the Alzheimer's Society; Joy Mead is a writer in Buckinghamshire; John Davies is a priest in Liverpool; Yvonne Morland, who has had a wide experience of working with people on the margins of society, is a poet and writer in Edinburgh.

I hope you enjoy this little book and that it helps you to look for God where you are. God is everywhere: on the isle of Iona and in the middle of Glasgow, in Guguletu and in Buckinghamshire; in friend and in stranger; in the church and in the world …

Neil Paynter
Epiphany, 2006,
Biggar, Scotland

* Cul Shuna is a house in Baile Mor (Iona village) where many Iona Community volunteers stay.

PALM SUNDAY

Leith Fisher

BIBLE READING

When they were approaching Jerusalem, at Bethphage and Bethany, near the Mount of Olives, he sent two of his disciples and said to them, 'Go into the village ahead of you, and immediately as you enter it, you will find tied there a colt that has never been ridden; untie it and bring it. If anyone says to you, "Why are you doing this?" just say this, "The Lord needs it and will send it back here immediately."' They went away and found a colt tied near a door, outside in the street. As they were untying it, some of the bystanders said to them, 'What are you doing, untying the colt?' They told them what Jesus had said; and they allowed them to take it. Then they brought the colt to Jesus and threw their cloaks on it; and he sat on it. Many people spread their cloaks on the road, and others spread leafy branches that they had cut in the fields. Then those who went ahead and those who followed were shouting,

> 'Hosanna!
> Blessed is the one who comes in the name of the Lord!
> Blessed is the coming kingdom of our ancestor David!
> Hosanna in the highest heaven!'

Then he entered Jerusalem and went into the temple; and when he had looked around at everything, as it was already late, he went out to Bethany with the twelve.

MARK 11:1–11 (NRSV)

REFLECTION

What *is* he playing at? The question is provoked by Mark's account of Jesus' entry into Jerusalem on the day we call Palm Sunday. Throughout Mark's story, to this point, Jesus has strenuously refused to go public on 'who he is'. Now, as he enters Jerusalem for the crucial confrontation which will end and begin around a cross on a hill and an empty tomb in a garden, he engineers a 'play' as he makes careful and elaborate preparations for what has been called a piece of 'street theatre'.

A demonstration is staged with the help of a borrowed donkey. In the highly charged atmosphere of the start of the week of Passover, Jesus enters the city on the donkey's back surrounded by the group of Galilean pilgrims with whom he has been travelling. Jesus and his followers come to the city by way of the Mount of Olives, evoking the words of the prophet Zechariah:

'For I will gather all the nations against Jerusalem to battle, and the city will be taken and the houses looted and the women raped: … Then the Lord will go forth and fight against these nations as when he fights on a day of battle. On that day his feet will stand on the Mount of Olives …' ZECHARIAH 14:2–4 (NRSV)

These words speak of a Messiah of the battles, making war on behalf of his people at the worst of times. However, the picture of Jesus on the back of the donkey poses the direct negative to the image of the warrior Messiah. Again the words are from Zechariah:

'Rejoice greatly, O daughter Zion!

Shout aloud, O daughter Jerusalem!

Lo! your king comes to you;

triumphant and victorious is he,

humble and riding on a donkey …

He will cut off the chariot from Ephraim

and the war horse from Jerusalem;

and the battle bow shall be cut off,

and he shall command peace to the nations.

ZECHARIAH 9: 9,10 (NRSV)

These words also speak about the liberation of Jerusalem, but the tone is far from militaristic. They speak of a Messiah who will bring liberation by another way, who comes in peace. Which is the way of Jesus?

In the events which will be unfolded in the coming week, the world and the disciples of Jesus alike will finally have revealed to them the answer to the crucial question of 'who he is'. This is no simple festal procession. The air is heavy with irony, contradiction, questioning. Dramatically, Jesus poses the question which will be fully answered on the bloody throne of Calvary's cross and in the mystery of a returning presence.

Mark's gospel frequently summons disciples to attention. We are bid 'look', 'listen', 'see'. The Palm Sunday 'play' of profound seriousness calls us to a yet deeper level of attentiveness. In the imminent journey to and through Good Friday we will finally learn 'who he is,' and our understanding of God and ourselves will never be the same again.

PRAYER

On the road to Jerusalem, Jesus,
you have spoken again and again
of your end and new beginning
to disciples who do not or will not understand.
Now you have entered the city
and you summon all who would follow you
to wait and watch with you.

Help us to enter into the intensity

of the week ahead of us

that we may truly wait and watch with you

as all is revealed, all is changed.

Before the revealing of love's way,

love's cost,

love's victory

and love's glory

may our lives be changed and reborn also.

Amen

QUESTIONS

Imagine yourself as an interested bystander as Jesus enters Jerusalem.

▶ What questions would you want to ask his disciples about him?

▶ What would you want to ask Jesus himself?

▶ What questions does the Palm Sunday event raise and leave with you?

MONDAY

Jan Sutch Pickard

When he came in sight of the city, he wept over it and said, 'If only you had known this day the way that leads to peace! But no; it is hidden from your sight. For a time will come upon you, when your enemies will set up siege-works against you; they will encircle you and hem you in at every point; they will bring you to the ground, you and your children within your walls, and not leave you one stone standing on another, because you did not recognise the time of God's visitation.'

LUKE 19:41–44 (REB)

If only.

If only you had known, had recognised, had accepted,

had believed in, had worked out how to live in

the way that leads to peace. If only.

If only we could recognise it.

If only we could find the courage to walk that way together.

But, seeing what has happened instead,

it's only human to weep,

over the city: the place where people live closely together –

but in fact the place where they can't live together,

where peace is an empty word. If only.

I wrote this just after returning home from Jerusalem after a three-month place-ment in the West Bank with the Ecumenical Accompaniment Programme in Palestine and Israel (EAPPI). If Jesus were to look out from the Mount of Olives today over that divided and disputed city, he would still weep. He would weep when confronted by the Wall, the separation barrier around the West Bank, coming between Bethlehem and Jerusalem, and cutting through the lives of thousands of Palestinians.

I believe God is weeping now over Israel and Palestine: over men without jobs, homes demolished, women mourning, families divided, babies born at checkpoints. Weeping over a century of conflict, of cautious co-existence, colonial rule, international intrigue, promises by politicians, meeting after meeting, hopes raised, hopes dashed; over persecuted people yearning for a place to call home, Jewish families who made the journey of a lifetime, a journey of faith; over a disaster in which thousands of Arab families lost their homes and still, nearly sixty years on, scattered around the Middle East, live as refugees.

Weeping about wars over territory, violence over ownership of 'holy places'; weeping because the Occupation has lasted for nearly 40 years; weeping for the attempts to shake it off, for children throwing stones, men living by the gun, people living in fear, with prejudice; young Israeli men and women confused by, misusing the power of uniform and weapons; desperate young Palestinian men and women who destroy themselves and complete strangers because they see no other way. Weeping for politicians on both sides: politicians with no real power to change things, politicians whose power is reinforced by foreign funding; weeping for the complicity of people like ourselves thousands of miles away; weeping for a situation that continues because of the world's apathy.

God weeps over what people are doing to each other. These are people who, in their heart of hearts, through their common humanity, know there is another way. Their daily greetings to each other – *Shalom, Salaam* – both mean Peace; they yearn for peace for their families; many wish that they could live in peace with their neighbours. But they are betrayed by their own history, and they have become hostages of world politics. In their anger, hurt, disillusion, despair they can no longer find or follow the way that leads to peace. And they have no tears left. How can we not weep at this? God is weeping for us all.

PRAYER

Weeping God,
you came to share our lives,
and still you share the vulnerability,
the suffering and desolation
of human beings in the land
that we call Holy,
and in many other places
made holy by your presence.

May we recognise your presence
amid each mess we've made;
give us your painful blessing of tears
for all we've done
and all we cannot prevent.
In the salt of tears
may we taste our common humanity;
and, through them, help us to see
the way that leads to peace.

QUESTIONS

▶ Where do you feel God is weeping, in other places in the world just now?

▶ What can you do to express your common humanity with the people in that place?

▶ What in your own country, community or family life might make God weep?

▶ In these situations, can you see the ways that lead to peace?

▶ What are they?

▶ What would be the first steps?

TUESDAY

Tom Gordon

BIBLE READING

Jesus and those who followed came to Jerusalem. And Jesus entered the temple and began to drive out those who were selling and those who were buying in the temple, and he overturned the tables of the money changers and the seats of those who sold doves; and he would not allow anyone to carry anything through the temple. He was teaching and saying, 'Is it not written, "My house shall be called a house of prayer for all the nations"? But you have made it a den of robbers.' And when the chief priests and the scribes heard it, they kept looking for a way to kill him; for they were afraid of him, because the whole crowd was spellbound by his teaching. And when evening came, Jesus and his disciples went out of the city.

MARK 11:15–19 (NRSV)

REFLECTION

Rachel's husband was dying in the hospice, and she was distraught with grief. There was no prospect of any meaningful life for her when her husband died. Life would not be worth living without him. The journey to death was distressing enough. The aftermath of his death was too horrendous to comprehend. Such was her faith that she turned to her church for comfort and reassurance. But worship, which once brought her strength, gave her little consolation. The hymns, which she once sung with vigour, now made her too emotional. The content of the liturgy, once a joy in its familiarity, was empty of meaning. She had become uncomfortable in her church. It was, she said, an alien place. And God had abandoned her too. Her prayers were dry. Her isolation was total. So she went to her priest for support, for she needed someone to help her make sense of what was happening in her life, in her church, and with her God, and her priest, surely, would understand.

'Why is this happening to me?' she asked her priest, at the door of the church after Sunday worship. 'Why this pain and suffering? How can I feel good about the church again? Why is my husband dying when he is the love of my life? How can I find hope when there is no hope? Where is God when I need him the most?'

And her priest smiled, and said, 'Now, now, it can't be that bad. And anyway, it's all part of God's plan, and we just have to be patient and wait for understanding to come.'

Rachel was crying when she told me her story. She had her fists clenched, and her knuckles were white. She was distressed and she was angry. 'What did you say back to your priest?' I asked, gently.

'Well, I'm only little, and, anyway, I was far too polite to punch her, so I said nothing, and went home, and took my anger out on my sitting room door – and I slammed it so hard I broke the glass!'

'Did it help?'

'You bet it did! I've never been so angry. Bloody priest, what kind of church does she want us to have? And see that God when I get hold of him? He'll get what-for as well.' And Rachel – feisty, angry, honest, real Rachel – smiled for the first times in ages.

My 'why?' is a question,

because it has a question mark at the end.

But it is no question, this 'why?',

for it has no answer,

no pat response to make it go away.

It is what it is –

a cry of pain,

a longing for peace,

a yearning for something to make sense.

So listen to my 'why?'

and accept me in my pain;

be with me in my distress,

and do not turn me aside.

For I am what I am

and that includes the 'why?'

My 'how?' is a query,

because it sounds like that when I say it.

But it is no query, this 'how?',

for it calls for no response,

no explanation to make it all come right.

It is what it is –

a fear for the future,

a passion for clarity,

a prayer for some hope again.

So be attentive to my 'how?'

and know me in my suffering;

wait with me in my anxiety,

and do not shut me out.

For I am what I need to be

and that includes the 'how?'

My rage is disturbing –

I know that, because it's not what you expect.

But it is real for me, this rage,

and needs not your pious judgement,

nor your rejection of this angry me.

It is what it is –

an anger at my God,

a rage at this injustice,

a fury at the suffering I must endure.

So understand this rage,

and be patient with my fury;

bear with me in my lashing out,

and do not bid me hush.

I need you now to know –

acceptance is your healing love for me.

So, listen to my 'why?',

for it drives out meek submission.

Be attentive to my 'how?',

for it overturns my passive faith.

Understand my angry rage

even though it makes you more afraid.

And come,

let us go on,

and find again what's true,

and tell again what's honest,

and know again what's real,

and wait again for hope

and healing love.

WEDNESDAY

Brian Woodcock

It was two days before the Passover and the festival of Unleavened Bread. The chief priests and the scribes were looking for a way to arrest Jesus by stealth and kill him; for they said, 'Not during the festival, or there may be a riot among the people.'

While he was at Bethany in the house of Simon the leper, as he sat at the table, a woman came with an alabaster jar of very costly ointment of nard, and she broke open the jar and poured the ointment on his head. But some were there who said to one another in anger, 'Why was the ointment wasted in this way? For this ointment could have been sold for more than three hundred denarii, and the money given to the poor.' And they scolded her. But Jesus said, 'Let her alone; why do you trouble her? She has performed a good service for me. For you always have the poor with you, and you can show kindness to them whenever you wish; but you will not always have me. She has done what she could; she has anointed my body beforehand for its burial. Truly I tell you, wherever the good news is proclaimed in the whole world, what she has done will be told in remembrance of her.'

Then Judas Iscariot, who was one of the twelve, went to the chief priests in order to betray him to them. When they heard it, they were greatly pleased, and promised to give him money. So he began to look for an opportunity to betray him.

On the first day of Unleavened Bread, when the Passover lamb is sacrificed, his disciples said to him, 'Where do you want us to go and make the preparations for you to eat the Passover?' So he sent two of his disciples, saying to them, 'Go into the city, and a man carrying a jar of water will meet you; follow him, and wherever he enters, say to the owner of the house, "The Teacher asks, Where is my guest room where I may eat the Passover with my disciples?" '

Mark 14: 1–11 (NRSV)

REFLECTION

'Why was the ointment wasted in this way? For this ointment could have been sold for more than three hundred denarii, and the money given to the poor.'

I was a wartime baby. Birthday presents were homemade, and the string and wrappings were saved for next time. We were not poor, but we had to be careful. There was always enough to eat, but whatever went on our bread was thinly spread, and the surplus scraped off again. And if I left anything on my dinner plate I would be reminded about the hungry children in the world.

We were very conscious of 'the poor'. At home I was given pocket money and taught to count my pennies. At church I would put one of them in a missionary box disguised as a little thatched hut, and was taught to count my blessings.

We were less sympathetic about 'the poor' in our town though. Such as the somewhat ostentatious funeral procession seen emerging from one of the more rundown areas, led by a horse-drawn hearse laden with flowers. We said flowers shouldn't be wasted on funerals, and thought the huge 'Our Charlie' in flowers on top of the coffin was just plain tasteless. 'Some of these folk aren't poor so much as wasteful!' I was told.

Then there was the report in our local paper of a man everyone thought was destitute, till he died and left a fortune. 'See?' we said. 'They pretend to be poor, but look what he was really worth!'

But all this began to confuse me. Did we care about the poor or not? I would gladly have given my cabbage to 'those in need', but that didn't seem to be the problem. What *was* the problem then? Saving or spending? Waste or taste?

It's a long time ago now of course. I have changed a lot since then. My parents changed too I think. So, come to that, did my church and its missionary boxes. But the story of Jesus at Bethany brings it all back.

Details of the story vary in the different gospels. Was the precious ointment poured on his head or his feet? Feet would have been less conspicuous – unless she really did wipe them with her hair, or, worse still, wash them with her tears. Feet might have given Jesus the same idea with his disciples a couple of days later: 'What she did I do; what I do you must do.' Head, on the other hand, would have really exceeded the bounds of good taste. Heads has it for Mark.

And who was the woman? Friend or stranger? Sinner or one of 'the poor'? She could afford expensive perfume. But maybe it was all she had. Her nest egg. Like the widow's mite – but a mite more costly. I can hear my father now! But there again, it is those with the least who have taught me the most about how to celebrate, and how to share, and the importance of doing both.

And who were her critics? Host or guests? The twelve disciples or just their treasurer, Judas? Not that it matters. They were probably all thinking the same thing anyway.

All except Jesus. That's the one thing the storytellers completely agree on. Jesus' bizarre response. Unperturbed. Unembarrassed. Practically revelling in it. As if this were one of the most significant things that had ever happened to him. As if her infatuation somehow didn't matter and her extravagance was fully justified. As if the whole incident should be recorded and proclaimed and made into history. Even if you can't make *poverty* history.

What no one tells us, because no one knew, is what *she* was thinking of. I bet it wasn't what *Jesus* was thinking! Yet somehow, inadvertently, she managed to mark his critical moment. And Jesus, for whom nothing happened by chance, turned it into a sign of the kingdom. Because that is what he always did. That was incarnation. For him everything was a revelation of God; all life a parable; each encounter divine. For him this was a celebration of the glory and tragedy of all that was about to happen. She had struck gold.

Jesus seemed genuinely grateful for her action. He wasn't going to let it be spoilt by guilt-making comments about 'the poor' – who, just then, she could have no more helped with her precious ointment than I could with my cabbage. This moment was special and unrepeatable: the honouring of a unique person who had done more for impoverished and marginalised people than any of his critics.

His critics would have their chance. 'The poor' would still be waiting for them next day. The question is, would the lessons of this special moment be taken on

board? – that *every* moment is special, *every* encounter unrepeatable, *every* person unique and to be honoured. That even the destitute have their worth. That everyone's life is worth celebrating, whether with flowers or costly ointment or a smile in the street.

If that is what is learnt as the story of the woman at Bethany is told and retold, then there is hope. Not for all 'the poor' at once maybe, but for real people, encounter by encounter, situation by situation, structure by unjust structure. And every time real people are given back their dignity Jesus is ministered to.

But her story carries a warning for those whose concern for 'the poor' falls short of real people. Or who only offer platitudes and generalisations. Or who claw back more in trade than they give in aid. The warning is this: When well-intentioned promises come to nothing, real people are betrayed. And their families, their communities and nations. And Jesus is betrayed again with them. That is the real waste: the waste of human possibility.

Prayer

Loving God, Creator,

you are far more generous than we know how to be.

Like a father

greeting his prodigal son who had wasted the family inheritance:

you run to meet us;

you lavish yet more upon us;

you welcome us back home.

Like a woman

pouring out her priceless perfume:

you bathe us in blessings

and replenish us with the riches of your grace.

Make us more receptive to your extravagance!

And less embarrassed by it.

We are so cautious, so calculating.

You hold nothing back.

You long to give us life; all of life there is.

Pour into us, then,

something of your generosity;

your spontaneity;

your reckless, unconditional love.

Make us into candidates for transformation,

agents of uncalculating generosity in the world.

Help us free things up.

Help us break open the gospel we carry around

all bottled up in ourselves and our churches.

Help us break it open and let it flow.

Good news for the poor! Freedom for the captives!

Life in abundance! For real and for all!

Help us anoint your body, not for dying but for living,

in what we do for others

and in who we are ourselves.

QUESTIONS FOR REFLECTION

▶ What am I best able to give to others?

>   What prevents me?
>   What might help me?

And what am I *least* able to give?

▶ What am I best able to receive from others?

>   What prevents me?
>   What might help me?

And what am I *least* able to receive?

▶ Am I more comfortable with giving or receiving?

▶ Do I learn anything from the story of Jesus at Bethany that might help
the way I live?

QUESTIONS FOR DISCUSSION

▶ Same as before: Do *we* learn anything from the story of Jesus at Bethany
that might help the way *we* live?

▶ How do we balance prudence and generosity as we relate to, for instance,
family and friends, strangers, community, work, the world, the planet?

MAUNDY THURSDAY

Peter Millar

BIBLE READING

LUKE 22:1–65 (GNB)

Prayer

Lord of every pilgrim heart,

may I journey with You today

remembering those

who plotted against You;

who betrayed You;

who shared the Passover with You;

who argued with You about who came first with God;

who denied You;

who prayed with You;

who left You alone;

who arrested You;

who denied You again;

who beat You and mocked You –

that my own life may again

be propelled to a deeper understanding

of the One who holds us all,

through Your surprising Spirit,

alive in our midst.

During the years when I had the privilege of working at Iona Abbey I always felt that Maundy Thursday was celebrated in an amazingly rich and meaningful way. We would begin in a crowded Abbey refectory by singing some of the wonderfully relevant and challenging Iona hymns (which now touch hearts around the world) followed by a symbolic washing of feet. Then, in the beauty of that restored room, with its stout walls and glorious roof, we would silently share the bread and the wine. Few words were spoken but the refectory that evening held a thousand emotions.

Then – again in silence – we would make our way to the dark cloisters to watch a short drama reminding us of the extraordinary events of the day before Jesus was killed. And from the cloisters we slowly walked into the Abbey church. We stood quietly in the darkness as, one by one, the candles were extinguished and the cross covered or taken away. All was ready for the morrow.

And then a total silence enveloped us as we just stood – held in God's wide embrace – and together were caught up in a mystery two thousand years old. And more than once in that great Maundy Thursday silence I heard a pilgrim's tears, reminding me of the mystery and wonder of our human condition.

Some stayed in the Abbey church long into the night, often reflecting not just on themselves but on our beautiful yet violent and divided world. One by one, or so it seemed, we went from that sacred place, permeated with the prayers

of the centuries, into the often wild Hebridean night. Our hearts had been moved by a power far beyond ourselves as we re-imagined the events of that first Maundy Thursday. Once again, the fragile yet ever present Spirit of the One who still suffers so much on our behalf had taken us all to a deeper place. A place articulated in this Gaelic traditional prayer:

> *Each thing we have received,*
> *from you it came, O God.*
> *Each thing for which we hope,*
> *from your love it will be given.*

As you read this, you are not likely to be on the windswept island of Iona, but I invite you to take ten or fifteen minutes from the rush of the day to sit quietly on this day before Good Friday. Try to let go of your many inner concerns and burdens. Relax. Breathe deeply. Make a space in your life. Do it deliberately, even if you are absolutely convinced that the phone call cannot wait and the e-mails must be read. (They will still be there in 15 minutes!) Be at one with yourself. Be 'centred in your heart', as many teachers of spirituality remind us. As the poster says: 'Let go and let God.'

And, as you experience even a brief sense of inner peace, slowly re-read some of these verses in Luke's gospel (chapter 22), which is a part of the Bible often read on this day of Holy Week. It's a wonderful passage, revealing so much about Jesus, about his companions, and about all of us in this world of many contradic-

tions and unexpected turnings. It's a passage brimming over with a range of emotions. It's high drama, but it's also an accurate mirror of ourselves. Who cannot identify him or herself with Peter's vociferous denial of Christ? And who has not known betrayal or been a betrayer? It's all here in these verses – the human condition in its myriad complexity!

It is a long passage, and I am reflecting here on only a few verses, but I encourage you to read it slowly in its entirety. All of our thoughts are important to God. Here are a few of mine relating to this text:

The chief priests and the teachers of the Law were afraid of the people, and so they were trying to find a way of putting Jesus to death secretly. (22:2)

Reflection: Let us remember all those who are at this very moment being silenced in many countries because they have witnessed to the truth; and the many groups throughout the world who bring their plight to our minds.

SILENCE

Judas agreed to take the money and started looking for a good chance to hand Jesus over to them without the people knowing about it. (22:6)

Reflection: What kinds of betrayals are taking place in our modern world? Are we colluding?

SILENCE

Then Jesus took a cup, gave thanks to God, and said, 'Take this and share it among yourselves. I tell you that from now on I will not drink this wine until the Kingdom of God comes.' Then he took the bread, gave thanks to God, broke it, and gave it to them, saying, 'This is my body, which is given for you. Do this in memory of me.' In the same way, he gave them the cup after the supper, saying, 'This cup is God's new covenant sealed with my blood, which is poured out for you.' (22:17–19)

Reflection: The church on earth and in heaven is always a sacred mystery. When it loses the 'sense of mystery' at its heart it becomes less and less aware of the Spirit's many unexpected surprises.

SILENCE

Jesus said to them: 'Who is greater, the one who sits down to eat or the one who serves? The one who sits down, of course. But I am among you as one who serves.' (22:27)

Reflection: Let us pause and pray for all those who today walk alongside the marginalised and weary. And for all those who through no fault of their own are the victims of our global exploitation.

SILENCE

'I tell you, Peter,' Jesus said, 'the cock will not crow tonight until you have said three times that you do not know me.' (22:34)

Prayer: Lord Christ, enable me to place my trust in you, and to live in the present moment. So often I deny you and reject your peace in which the healing of my mind and heart are earthed. Yet your song pierces even my darkest days, and your friendship is always the source of my journey into wholeness.[1]

SILENCE

Rising from his prayer, he went back to the disciples and found them asleep, worn out by their grief. He said to them, 'Why are you sleeping? Get up and pray that you will not fall into temptation.' (22:45–46)

Reflection: It's more than easy to go to sleep; to lose both faith and hope in God and in others. There is a prayer from the Philippines which has always inspired me to start again:

Lord, when we fear we are losing hope or feel that our efforts are futile, let us see in our hearts and minds the image of your resurrection, and let that be our source of courage and strength.

SILENCE

Jesus said to the chief priests and officers of the temple guard and the elders who had come to get him, 'Did you have to come with swords and clubs, as though I were an outlaw? I was with you in the temple every day, and you did not try to arrest me. But this is your hour to act, when the power of darkness rules.' (22:52–53)

Reflection: Almost every day we hear or read of such arrests. Women, men and children who are the victims of appalling and ongoing injustice. Taken in the dark. Often tortured. Brutally murdered. That is why it is so important that those of us who experience relative security in our lives do not remain silent, even if speaking out brings pain into our own life.

SILENCE

The Lord turned round and looked straight at Peter, and Peter remembered that the Lord had said to him, 'Before the cock crows tonight, you will say three times that you do not know me.' Peter went out and wept bitterly. (22:61–62)

Reflection: One of the amazing things in our world today is that Christ is often powerfully present among those who suffer so desperately. Millions of those who live in terrible situations know at the deepest level of their being that God is with them in it all. When I meet such folk I feel that they have had the experience of looking straight into the face of Jesus, as Peter did on that fateful night. Is such a possibility open to us?

SILENCE

The men who were guarding Jesus mocked him and beat him. They blindfolded him and asked him, 'Who hit you? Guess!' And they said many other insulting things to him. (22:63–65)

Reflection: As I grow older I know one thing for certain. The God who I try to follow is at the heart of human suffering. Not looking on, but weeping with us. This can sound trite, but I know it from personal experience. We are not abandoned when the dark night overtakes us. Generations ago they expressed that truth with such clarity in this wonderful prayer from our Celtic heritage:

God be with thee in every pass,
Jesus be with thee on every hill,
Spirit be with thee in every stream,
Headland ridge and moor.

Each sea and land, each path and meadow,
Each lying down, each rising up,
In the trough of the waves,
On the crest of the billows,
Each step of the journey thou goest.

1. Adapted from a prayer in *An Iona Prayer Book*, Peter Millar, Canterbury Press. p 41.

GOOD FRIDAY

Kathy Galloway

BIBLE READING

It was about twelve o'clock when the sun stopped shining and darkness covered the whole country until three o'clock; and the curtain hanging in the temple was torn in two. Jesus cried out in a loud voice, 'Father! In your hands I place my spirit!' He said this and died.

The army officer saw what had happened, and he praised God, saying, 'Certainly he was a good man!'

When the people who had gathered there to watch the spectacle saw what happened, they all went back home, beating their breasts in sorrow. All those who knew Jesus personally, including the women who had followed him from Galilee, stood at a distance to watch.

LUKE 23:44-49 (GNB)

REFLECTION

Every time I hear the gospel account of the crucifixion of Jesus, I am struck by how familiar it all is. Of course that is partly because I have followed it every Holy Week since my own childhood; it threads its way through my life. But it is also a story that I see and hear every day of the week in the world that I live in, reported on television and in newspapers, played out in the lives of contemporaries. The brutal and horrible torture, the judicial execution of the innocent by power under threat, the moral authority of such death to move bystanders, the senti-mental crowd, at one moment adulatory, at the next malevolent, at the next sorrowful, the friends who watch and weep from a distance, and all of it a spec-tacle to be watched and commented on – all of this is as old as the hills and as new as the latest news from Iraq or the Middle East or Sudan. It is the wearily familiar story of suffering. There is nothing unique about crucifixion.

Within the gospel Good Friday of many stories, two in particular stand out for me. One is characterised by presence and compassion; the other is characterised by absence and silence.

The first is a story of accompaniment. It is the story of those who loved Jesus, his community of friends and family. It is about the women who had followed Jesus from Galilee and provided for him, who had anointed him for death, who had

accompanied him on the way of the cross and watched from a distance as he suffered his terrible agony and death. It is about that good man of means, Joseph of Arimathea, himself wrapping Jesus' body in a linen sheet and laying him in his own tomb, and it's about that other good man, Nicodemus, giving of his substance so that Jesus might have a decent burial according to custom. It's about John, the beloved disciple, and Mary, the mother of Jesus, giving comfort to one another; it's about women weeping together, and watching where Jesus was laid. It's about Mary Magdalene, watching and waiting.

This story of presence and compassion, of accompaniment in suffering, of just being there, doing small, ordinary, important practical things, is one that we in the Iona Community have had the privilege of observing in the JL Zwane Presbyterian Church in Guguletu, South Africa. This is a church which has made a faith-filled decision to have a ministry of presence and compassion to people living with HIV/AIDS in that community; a huge commitment in a township where the infection rate is something like 25%, many people live in extreme poverty, and the kind of treatment available in the West is either too expensive or just unavailable.

We have so much to learn from this model of accompaniment, not least from its holistic nature, which cares for the whole person and engages a whole community. But being alongside people in compassion and care, does not only happen in Guguletu. It happens wherever people stand beside others in solidarity, watch

through long nights with them, prepare food for those too weary or ill or despairing to do it themselves, look after the children for a while, read to a friend or simply offer an encouraging word or smile or hug or shoulder to lean on. It happens when people respect another's wishes, preserve their confidences, protect their need for solitude or privacy, refrain from telling them how to solve their problems or live their lives. This ministry of presence and compassion is not the particular preserve of Christians, or of any one nationality or culture. It is perhaps the best flowering of our mutual humanity, the highest regard that human beings can offer one another.

And yet ... at its heart is a kind of powerlessness. It is the powerlessness of people in Guguletu in the face of a catastrophically unjust world economic order which puts uncalculable resources into protecting the interests and profits of the powerful of the world and almost nothing by comparison into overcoming poverty and preventable or treatable disease. It is the powerlessness of being confronted with violence at every level – irrational, intractable, unpredictable in its outcome, breeding only more violence. It is the powerlessness of a mother watching her child die, or indeed anyone we love die. It is the powerlessness of our own inadequacy and frailty in the face of the deep hurt of others, in the face of all that we cannot prevent or solve. It is the powerlessness of Mary and John and Joseph of Arimathea and Nicodemus and Mary Magdalene. Because there is the other story, the story of absence and silence.

The story of presence and compassion is inextricably linked to that other story of suffering and death. But it is not the same. Where Jesus went now, his friends could not follow. This is the silence of isolation, the absence of a different place.

> *Jesus walked this lonesome valley, he had to walk it by himself;*
> *O nobody else could walk it for him, he had to walk it by himself.*
> (AMERICAN SPIRITUAL)

In the face of the mystery of human suffering, the other authentic response, along with compassion, is silence. None of us can really describe what the reality of suffering is for another. To keep silent is not to minimise or disrespect another's suffering, far less to be complacent in the face of it, or to believe that we are thereby relieved of the need to keep working to overcome all that causes preventable suffering. It is rather to recognise that suffering and death are part of the human condition; indeed, they are the only inescapable part.

TS Eliot famously said that human beings cannot bear very much reality, and perhaps that is why we have so many stories or theologies about suffering and death, some of which are bleak indeed, all of which are ultimately inadequate. And the ruthlessness of the executioners, the moral recognition of the bystanders, the sentimentality of the crowd, the excitability (and, sometimes, the sadism) of the commentators, even the compassion of the accompaniers, are all also ultimately inadequate to save us from the reality of suffering and death.

You must go and stand your trial, you have to stand it by yourself

O nobody else can stand it for you, you have to stand it by yourself

We who are Christians give a special meaning to the suffering and death of Jesus. We recognise that beyond all our evasions and explanations, it has the capacity to confront us with the absolute certainty of death. *'The memory of that which is intolerable to us is remembered in Christ's body, in which is named all the violence of the world … the broken and unremembered victims of tyranny and sin.'* (Janet Morley) The absence and silence of Christ's death bring us face to face not only with our own profoundest grief, but with the reality of all suffering, all evil, all pity and sorrow. The cross is a symbol of all that the worst of human violence and fear can do to goodness and innocence. But, beyond even that, it is the entry into the depths of my own potential for violence and corruption, into my nameless imaginings and my darkest fears of punishment, betrayal, abandonment, and the terror of the unknown; into the destruction of all life and love. Even to stand unprotected beside the cross for a moment is almost unbearable. *'My God, my God, why did you abandon me?'*

But confronted with our powerlessness in the face of death, behold, here is a mystery! In embracing the reality of death, there is a gift of enormous power and agency. Can it be that the power of transformation is most active, is strongest, precisely in the absence and the silence? That is a question for another day.

In the meantime, we live with two Good Friday narratives side by side. The first speaks of the tasks of compassion and presence.

> *My heart is moved by all I cannot save:*
> *so much has been destroyed.*
>
> *I have to cast my lot with those*
> *who, age after age, perversely,*
>
> *with no extraordinary power*
> *reconstitute the world.*
>
> (ADRIENNE RICH, FROM 'NATURAL RESOURCES')

The second is the narrative of absence and silence

Though hope desert my heart,
though strangeness fill my soul,
though truth torment my troubled mind,
you have been here before.

Though confidence run dry,
though weary flesh be sore,
though conversation bear no fruit,
you have been here before

There is no threatening place,
no trial I could know
which has not known your presence first:
you have been here before.

I will not dread the dark,
the fate beyond control,
nor fear what reigns in frightening things:
you will be there before.

(JOHN L BELL, FROM 'YOU HAVE BEEN HERE BEFORE')

HOLY
SATURDAY

Ruth Burgess

God's steadfast love endures for ever

PSALM 118:1 (NRSV, inclusive version)

He is not here

MARK 16:6 (NRSV)

REFLECTION

He is not here.

So where is he?

Tradition tells us that Jesus spent the hours
between the crucifixion and the resurrection
harrowing the halls of Hell;
this is a popular tradition
celebrated in story and mystery play
from then till now,
the rap of Jesus on Hell's door
sending a shiver down the spine
of all who hear it.

Is that where he is?
Freeing the captives,
in death as in life,
bringing his people safely home?

I like the tradition.

As I grow older
I think more about death.
I am not sure what I believe about eternity.
The mystery grows deeper rather than clearer.
I am full of questions.

Today is a day of death.
Today we are given permission to mourn, to cry,
to wonder.
Today we are encouraged to be still.
To let God hold us in the silence.

So let's do it.
Let's take time out
from anticipating the resurrection,
to be with Jesus,
wherever he is.

From the Office Hymn for Holy Saturday (Stanbrook Abbey):

His cross stands empty in a world grown silent
Through hours of anguish and of dread;
In stillness, earth awaits the resurrection,
While Christ goes down to wake the dead.

He summons Adam and his generations,
Brings light where darkness endless seemed;
He frees and claims his own, so long held captive,
Who, with the living, are redeemed.

SUGGESTIONS FOR PRAYER

Spend time today in a cemetery or graveyard.
Tend the grave of a family member, a friend, or a stranger.

Give yourself time and permission to grieve:
for someone you love,
for lost opportunities,
for unfulfilled dreams.

Ask yourself:
What has or needs to die in me this year?
Who or what holds me captive?
What is God raising to life in me?
In my home? In my community?

Somewhere in your home, clean, oil or possibly paint a door.
Focus on the divine activity of opening and closing doors. Pray as you work.

Explore how the harrowing of Hell has been portrayed
in art, drama and story.

With the psalmist,
give thanks, because God's love is for ever.

EASTER SUNDAY

Joy Mead

BIBLE READING

Early on the first day of the week, while it was still dark, Mary of Magdala came to the tomb. She saw that the stone had been moved away from the entrance, and ran to Simon Peter and the other disciple, the one whom Jesus loved. 'They have taken the Lord out of the tomb,' she said, 'and we do not know where they have laid him.' So Peter and the other disciple set out and made their way to the tomb. They ran together, but the other disciple ran faster than Peter and reached the tomb first. He peered in and saw the linen wrappings lying there, but he did not enter. Then Simon Peter caught up with him and went into the tomb. He saw the linen wrappings lying there, and the napkin which had been round his head, not with the wrappings but rolled up in a place by itself. Then the disciple who had reached the tomb first also went in, and saw and believed; until then they had not understood the scriptures, which showed that he must rise from the dead.

So the disciples went home again; but Mary stood outside the tomb weeping. And as she wept, she peered into the tomb, and saw two angels in white sitting there, one at the head, and one at the feet, where the body of Jesus had lain. They asked her, 'Why are you weeping?' She answered, 'They have taken my Lord away, and I do not know where they have laid him.' With these words she turned round and saw Jesus standing there, but she did not recognise him.

Jesus asked her, 'Why are you weeping? Who are you looking for?' Thinking it was the gardener, she said, 'If it is you, sir, who removed him, tell me where you have laid him, and I will take him away.' Jesus said, 'Mary!' She turned and said to him, 'Rabbuni!' (which is Hebrew for 'Teacher'). 'Do not cling to me,' said Jesus, 'for I have not yet ascended to the Father. But go to my brothers, and tell them that I am ascending to my Father and your Father, to my God and your God.' Mary of Magdala went to tell the disciples. 'I have seen the Lord!' she said, and gave them his message.

Late that same day, the first day of the week, when the disciples were together behind locked doors for fear of the Jews, Jesus came and stood among them. 'Peace be with you!' he said; then he showed them his hands and his side. On seeing the Lord the disciples were overjoyed. Jesus said again, 'Peace be with you! As the Father sent me, so I send you.' Then he breathed on them, saying, 'Receive the Holy Spirit! If you forgive anyone's sins, they are forgiven; if you pronounce them unforgiven, unforgiven they remain.'

JOHN 20:1–23 (REB)

'Early on the first day of the week, while it was still dark, Mary of Magdala came to the tomb' – the haunting opening words of a strange and beautiful story. It begins in a garden in the deep dark just before the dawn. This story is elemental, still holding within it remnants of pagan beliefs. The earth is waiting. In the darkness of the soil seeds of new life await the coming of light. In the sowing and the wanting, the caring and the waiting we are one with seeds and growing things. We know resurrection every time green bursts out of the winter dark, buds open, daffodils yellow the earth.

The story is also human, full of emotion. John chooses his images carefully. There is a poetic sense of the decisiveness of details: like Mary mistaking Jesus for the gardener. The stone that holds those things we thought we knew – our dogmas and creeds, our theories and theologies – has been rolled away and we are left with empty space we must learn to love, uncertainties we must learn to live with. Angels give a different light to things as they encourage us to trust in this new dawning.

Later (in verses 19–23) we are taken out of the garden to a room with 'locked doors' and a gathering of bewildered disciples. The image of breath and breathing is powerful. Jesus hasn't left his friends with a book of rules but with the feel of his breath on them and the memory of meals together. (There are many stories about Jesus and meals. Shouldn't this remind us that every meal shared is a resurrection story?) Creative remembering keeps the disciples' spirit-filled feet

firmly on the ground. Life-giving, forgiving (see verse 23) and connecting energy builds community, awakens imagination, enables them to think 'out of the box', outside 'locked doors'.

Now, no learned discussion or research, no presentation of contrived evidence, no amount of listening to daft sermons and whimsical homilies, no muttering about mystery, will make me believe that large boulders roll about on their own, dead bodies walk and talk, angels are tangible shiny beings dressed in white linen. Applying my reasoning faculties (such as they are!) to this story is a huge waste of time. I don't believe it and I don't want to believe it. I don't even think meaning matters here. It's not a story to explain, it's a story to live by. Reading or telling stories is about a lot more than what I do or don't believe. It has to do with poetic sensibility and liberated imagination – prophetic imagination, perhaps. Story-telling is resurrection – and resurrection, somebody once said, is a laugh freed for ever and ever.

I listened recently to a speaker expressing the need to pare away all that is unnecessary, all we can't believe or accept in the Jesus stories so that we get to the truth. What truth? I wondered. Whose truth? This seems to be dangerous stuff. The images a storyteller or poet uses are not ornaments that can be discarded at will. They are the truths of the story and there to be pondered with open hearts and minds.

In his obituary for Brother Roger of Taizé, Alain Woodrow, writing in *The Guardian*, said, '*Taizé's success lies in its idealism. It is not liberal or conservative, Catholic or Protestant. It is idealistic. Its strength is in the poetry of its message, open to any interpretation.*'[1] Isn't resurrection pure poetry? All who tell and re-tell stories, from gospel writer to grandmother with a child on her knee, have a responsibility not to pollute stories by promoting their own interests. Stories must be allowed to go free. To tell stories is to trust in life, to hope.

In *Zebra and Other Stories,* by the Jewish writer Chaim Potok, one of the characters notes, '*I think losing your soul is when you can't tell a story about something that has happened to you.*' So in sharing stories we are sharing what rises from our deepest being. I know deep within me that resurrection happens, in the same way as I know love strong enough to go to a cross happens. I don't believe John's story but I do believe *in* it. I believe in the dark in which seeds grow. I believe in the sunrise of hope. We are not told of the sun's rising in John's story. Like Mary, we take a while to realise what is happening. Then we begin to see the light, to imagine the warmth of the sun's rays, new life and a new day, an unexplainable heart-warming as things emerge in outline, then fill with colour.

Colour, beauty, shape depend not only on the source of light but upon our capacity to receive the light, to see into the heart of things, to let new thoughts, new hopes, dawn *upon* us. John creates a story to live by out of the stuff of our

humanness. I believe in forgiveness. I believe in the unlimited potency of imagination and the people's dreams. When strangers share stories, when someone lays a hand on your arm and holds your attention – like Coleridge's ancient Mariner – that's a resurrection moment.

We are all characters in a once-upon-a-time sort of story and carry within us warnings, lessons, wisdom … and hope. Stories are about our hunger for life itself. Sometimes we need a story more than food and as we need good food we need good stories. *'Words'*, Ben Okri tells us, *'collect in the blood, in the soul and either transform or poison people's lives'.* [2]

After the attacks on the World Trade Centre on 11th September, 2001 and the London Underground on 7th July, 2005, there were long moments when almost everyone and everything seemed to pause – a sort of Holy Saturday space when things could move towards love or hate, towards despair or hope. There was an opening, a chance which ordinary people (in resistance to government) grasped. They talked to strangers. Resurrection stories of fragile heroes and ordinary people who refused to hate emerged out of the wreckage.

There was and still is at large in the world amazing imaginative power to reinvent ourselves. We can't say how it will work against corporate and government mindlessness and oppression. We know we are in the dark but perhaps that is a

good place to be, a good place from which to go on telling the people's hopes and dreams.

We need to tell again and again of millions of people around the world forming co-ops, campaign groups, self-help groups, organising protests and peace marches, seeking to Make Poverty History, seeking trade justice, seeking the end to oppression and social marginalisation. What is remarkable about all this is the opportunity for ordinary people to speak out, to participate, to share their hopes and dreams. And at the heart of their stories is love strong enough to banish fear and bear regrets. What do we expect to achieve? We don't know. We're still in the dark. But hope isn't about expectations – as the Jesus stories show us – it's about surprises! Transformation begins in imagination … in telling the story … in letting joy sneak in. People who live by the resurrection story are people of imagination, love, discernment, joy, hope … people in the dark who *feel* the coming of the dawn.

1. *The Guardian*, Friday, 19th August, 2005
2. From 'Beyond Words' in *A Way of Being Free*, Ben Okri, Phoenix House, London, 1997, p.88.

IONA DAWN

I am by the shore
in the early darkness
    when the rising sun
    touches a broken world,
    makes a flame
    of each blade of grass,
    warms the silent stones,
    sends larks up
    into the clean air.
The new day miracle
and the end of waiting:
I am emptied wholly
into a moment of trust
with no desire to make sense
of all this light.

ON THE ROAD

We Walked On to Emmaus
Luke 24:13–35

We walked on to Emmaus
with a man who came from nowhere
knowing nothing except that which he was told;
and his friendship was an excuse
for our telling of these tales,
which comforted us, though our hearts were cold.

We walked on to Emmaus
full of all the fondest memories
and our kindling of them made us feel more bold;
for the questions that he asked us
were bread to feed our thoughts,
and a comfort to us, though our hearts were cold.

We walked on to Emmaus
and we told him about Mary
giving some small hope to which our hearts could hold;

and we talked of resurrection

and the strange scene in the garden,

which comforted us, though our hearts were cold.

We walked on to Emmaus

and were shocked by his insistence

that all these things had been foreseen of old;

and the fire of his persistence

was bread which fed our souls:

a breaking fire which purged our hearts of cold.

John Davies

FISH

John 21:9–14

We found ourselves
sharing fish,
not by an open fire and a lake
but in a city basement
hours after the supper,
remembered original sacrament.

Flesh parted cleanly
(no blood or agony),
pink and delicious,
prepared by unseen hands,
detached from our concern,
a product for our use.

How easily we accept
the sacrifice of others;

cold nights at sea,

stretching timber,

nails tearing skin,

frayed ropes tightening.

In a simple meal

lies all the paradox

of a world consuming itself

head to tail

fish-eye swivelled

from scales falling unseen.

Yvonne Morland

POSTCARD FROM BILLY

Hallo! Anyone there on Iona still remember me?

Sorry I haven't written sooner. I've been on the road. Visited Kieran in Glasgow; Sarah and Mags in Liverpool. I'm living with Martina now in London. London's a great city. I've seen Jesus quite a few times here. In men, in children, in a homeless woman I was talking to on the Strand – even in my own family. Martina and I started an Iona worship group. We meet once a week and do Amnesty International letter writing afterwards.

It was hard leaving Iona but I'm doing OK. I miss it though. I'll probably always come back – if not physically, in my mind, in my heart – to connect.

Well, I hope you are all in good health. If you're ever in London look us up. Keep in touch.

Peace,
Love,

Billy

P.S. Say hallo to the north beach for me.

The Cross Stands Empty

The cross stands empty
stark, against the sky.
Our worst fears and predictions
are torn aside like a veil from the face.
We cannot but be joyful
for our hearts leap within us.
Sing in praise of forgiving love,
the love God has for all humanity.

Blessed be God whose mercy surrounds us.
Blessed be Jesus, the core of our hearts' longing.
Blessed be the Holy Spirit, our joy and liberation.

Yvonne Morland

SOURCES

Monday – Extract from *The Revised English Bible* © Oxford University Press and Cambridge University Press 1989. Used by permission.

Good Friday – 'You Have Been Here Before', words by John L Bell, © Wild Goose Resource Group, from *Church Hymnary*, 4th edition, Canterbury Press, 2005, ISBN 1853116130. Used by permission of John L Bell and the Wild Goose Resource Group.

Saturday – Office hymn for Holy Saturday from Stanbrook Abbey used by permission of Stanbrook Abbey.

Easter Sunday – Extract from *The Revised English Bible* © Oxford University Press and Cambridge University Press 1989. Used by permission.

Scriptures quoted from *The New Revised Standard Version of the Bible*, copyright © 1989, Division of Christian Education of the National Council of Churches of Christ in the USA. Used by permission. All rights reserved.

Scriptures quoted from *The NRSV* (inclusive version) version of the Bible from *The New Testament and Psalms: An inclusive version*, Oxford University Press, copyright 1995 Oxford University Press Inc.

Scriptures quoted from *The Good News Bible* published by The Bible Societies/Harper Collins Publishers Ltd., UK, © American Bible Society, 1966, 1971, 1976, 1992.

Cover photograph © Joy Mead

THE IONA COMMUNITY IS

- An ecumenical movement of men and women from different walks of life and different traditions in the Christian church
- Committed to the gospel of Jesus Christ, and to following where that leads, even into the unknown
- Engaged together, and with people of goodwill across the world, in acting, reflecting and praying for justice, peace and the integrity of creation
- Convinced that the inclusive community we seek must be embodied in the community we practise

Together with our staff, we are responsible for:

- Our islands residential centres of Iona Abbey, the MacLeod Centre on Iona, and Camas Adventure Centre on the Ross of Mull

and in Glasgow:

- The administration of the Community
- Our work with young people
- Our publishing house, Wild Goose Publications
- Our association in the revitalising of worship with the Wild Goose Resource Group

The Iona Community was founded in Glasgow in 1938 by George MacLeod, minister, visionary and prophetic witness for peace, in the context of the poverty and despair of the Depression. Its original task of rebuilding the monastic ruins of Iona Abbey became a sign of hopeful rebuilding of community in Scotland and beyond. Today, we are about 250 Members, mostly in Britain, and 1500 Associate Members, with 1400 Friends worldwide. Together and apart, 'we follow the light we have, and pray for more light'.

For information on the Iona Community contact:
The Iona Community, Fourth Floor, Savoy House, 140 Sauchiehall Street,
Glasgow G2 3DH, UK. Phone: 0141 332 6343
e-mail: ionacomm@gla.iona.org.uk; web: www.iona.org.uk

For enquiries about visiting Iona, please contact:
Iona Abbey, Isle of Iona, Argyll PA76 6SN, UK. Phone: 01681 700404
e-mail: ionacomm@iona.org.uk

Also from Wild Goose Publications ...

Lent & Easter Readings from Iona

Neil Paynter (ed)

This book of readings from members and staff of the Iona Community aims to help us reappraise our lives during the period leading up to Easter. Lent is traditionally a time of repentance and penitence but it also offers an opportunity to see the world afresh, with a new sense of wonder. These readings encourage us not only to regard ourselves with a healthy realism, so that we can accept responsibility for our shortcomings, but also to recognise the nature and purposes of God and the never-ending renewal of possibility, both within ourselves and in the world.

ISBN 1901557626

Eggs & Ashes

Practical & liturgical resources for Lent and Holy Week

Ruth Burgess & Chris Polhill

Modern, relevant resources to accompany readers through Lent and Easter for many years, with material for Shrove Tuesday, Ash Wednesday, Mothering Sunday, Palm Sunday and Holy Week: liturgies, responses, prayers, poems, reflections, meditations, stories, stations of the cross, sermons, monologues and songs, with some all-age resources, as well as suggestions for a Lent discipline for those who care about the environment.

ISBN 1901557871

www.ionabooks.com for online ordering

Stages on the Way
Worship Resources for Lent, Holy Week and Easter
Wild Goose Worship Group

This is the second 'book of bits' for worship produced by the Wild Goose Worship Group. It traces Jesus' road to the cross through Lent, Holy Week and Easter. Its prime purpose is to resource worship that enables people to sense the hope, apprehension and joy of Easter as felt by Jesus' friends. The range and diversity offers a unique source of elements for lay and clergy worship planners and enablers. All of the material has been used in celebrations and services of public worship, but little has been previously published.

ISBN 1901557111

Enemy of Apathy
Songbook
John L Bell/Graham Maule

Sixty-two songs and chants for Lent, Eastertide and Pentecost. Includes:
* Travelling the road to freedom
* Be still and know
* Jesus Christ is waiting
* Lord of the morning
* Kyrie/Sanctus & Benedictus/Agnus Dei (Kentigern setting)

ISBN 0947988270

More from Wild Goose Publications ...

This Is the Day
Neil Paynter (ed)

Daily readings for four months from a wide range of contributors within the Iona Community. These prayers, liturgies, songs, poems and articles, which reflect the concerns of the Community, can be used for group or individual reflection and are intended to inspire positive action and change in our lives. Subjects covered include: hospitality and welcome, justice and peace, the environment, healing, church renewal, worship, work, racial justice, pilgrimage, sexuality, Columban Christianity and the Celtic tradition, inferfaith dialogue, nonviolence and peace-keeping, spirituality, commitment, economic witness and more.

ISBN 1901557634

Blessed Be Our Table
Graces for mealtimes and reflections on food
Neil Paynter (ed)

This book integrates thankfulness with a burning passion for justice, both of which are central to our relationship with a bountiful provider God, with the whole wondrous creation, with each other, and with our sisters and brothers throughout the world who, because of greed and injustice, will not receive their daily bread today. Inviting us to recommit ourselves to act for justice each time we join in the simple sharing of a meal, it is also very much a celebration of food, of diversity, of community and sharing, of Creator and creation.

ISBN 1901557723